T0395350

Ocean
Animals

THIS EDITION
Editorial Management by Oriel Square
Produced for DK by WonderLab Group LLC
Jennifer Emmett, Erica Green, Kate Hale, *Founders*

Editors Grace Hill Smith, Libby Romero, Michaela Weglinski;
Photography Editors Kelley Miller, Annette Kiesow, Nicole DiMella;
Managing Editor Rachel Houghton; **Designers** Project Design Company;
Researcher Michelle Harris; **Copy Editor** Lori Merritt; **Indexer** Connie Binder;
Proofreader Larry Shea; **Reading Specialist** Dr. Jennifer Albro; **Curriculum Specialist** Flaine Larson

Published in the United States by DK Publishing
1745 Broadway, 20th Floor, New York, NY 10019

Copyright © 2023 Dorling Kindersley Limited
DK, a Division of Penguin Random House LLC
23 24 25 26 10 9 8 7 6 5 4 3 2 1
001-333980-June/2023

A catalog record for this book
is available from the Library of Congress.
HC ISBN: 978-0-7440-7297-6
PB ISBN: 978-0-7440-7298-3

DK books are available at special discounts when purchased in bulk for sales promotions, premiums, fundraising, or educational use. For details, contact: DK Publishing Special Markets,
1745 Broadway, 20th Floor, New York, NY 10019
SpecialSales@dk.com

Printed and bound in China

The publisher would like to thank the following for their kind permission to reproduce their images:
a=above; c=center; b=below; l=left; r=right; t=top; b/g=background

123RF.com: Visarute Angkatavanich 3cb, 20br; **Alamy Stock Photo:** Paul Harris 16-17, Paul Harris 16br;
Dorling Kindersley: Linda Pitkin 31clb; **Dreamstime.com:** Steve Allen 7tr, Andreykuzmin 20-21, Isselee 8br, Izanbar 14-15bc, Eugene Sim Junying 31cl, Neirfy 5tl, Sandra Nelson 11tr, Sandra Nelson 30cra, Stéphane Rochon 22-23;
Getty Images: 500px Prime / Grant Thomas 9tr; **Getty Images / iStock:** atese 22br, Dimitris66 31bl, Thierry Eidenweil 23cr, fenkieandreas 20c, Gwenvidig 17tc, ifish 27bl, ifish 31clb/1, Joegolby 10-11, Uz5 30ca, KPegg 9bc, Mlharing 11c, RomoloTavani 29br, Mireia Querol Rovira 17bc, tswinner 25br, Tatiana Dzhemileva 4-5; **Shutterstock.com:** Chris Allan 28br, 31tl, alonanola 13bl, Daniel Avram 5cr, Karel Bartik 4-5c, 10-11bc, Agung bayu 6-7bc, Beltsazar 6-7, Maciej Czekajewski 4bc, 7bc, 31bl/1, Divelvanov 12-13, DiveIvanov 18-19, David Evison 12bc, Leonardo Gonzalez 8-9, Shane Gross 25bl, Andrea Izzotti 24br, Jellyman Photography 15br, Patrik Jonson 4bl, 27bc, Tory Kallman 28-29, orifec_a31 30, orlandin 18br, SergeUWPhoto 26br, Shane Myers Photography 14-15, Sergey Teryaev 19bl, VisionDive 13bc, 31cla, Richard Whitcombe 1cb, wildestanimal 19cb, Wirestock Creators 9bl, Christian Wittmann 29bl, Mike Workman 26-27

Cover images: *Front:* **Dreamstime.com:** Noviantoko Tri Arijanto b, Iuliia Sutiagina b/g;
Getty Images / iStock: Bullet_Chained c, ca; **Shutterstock.com:** VectorShow cra;
Back: **Dreamstime.com:** Punnawich Limparungpatanakij cra; **Getty Images / iStock:** Bullet_Chained clb;
Spine: **Getty Images / iStock:** Bullet_Chained

All other images © Dorling Kindersley
For more information see: www.dkimages.com

For the curious
www.dk.com

Ocean
Animals

Ruth A. Musgrave

Many animals live in the ocean.
Meet some of them.

Race to the water with this baby sea turtle.
A bird is chasing it.
Go turtle go!

baby sea turtle

Ride the waves with
a sea lion.
Twist. Turn. Jump.
Watch out
for that
big wave!

sea lion

This bird dives into the water. It swims fast!

penguin

Swim with this fish. But you will have to find it first.

frogfish

whale shark

This big shark gulps
little fish.
Open wide.

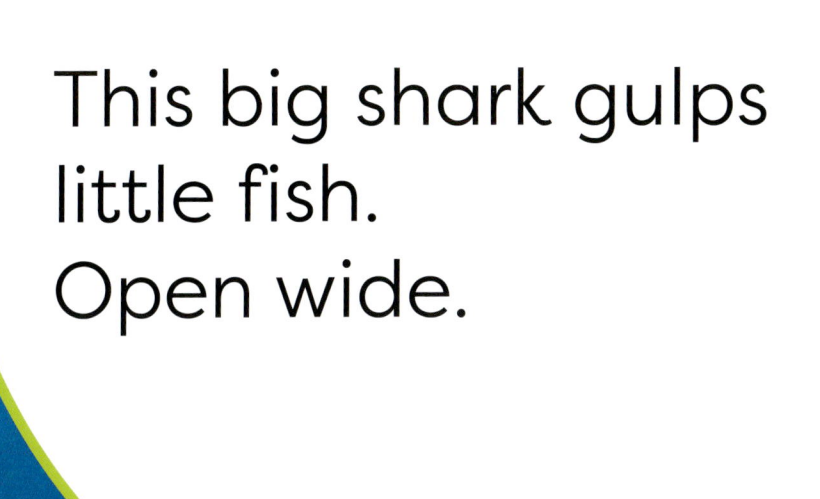

Set sail with this jelly.
It needs the wind to push it.
Blow wind blow!

by-the-wind sailor

nautilus

Look at this animal.
It has a big shell.
The shell helps it
go up.
Then down.

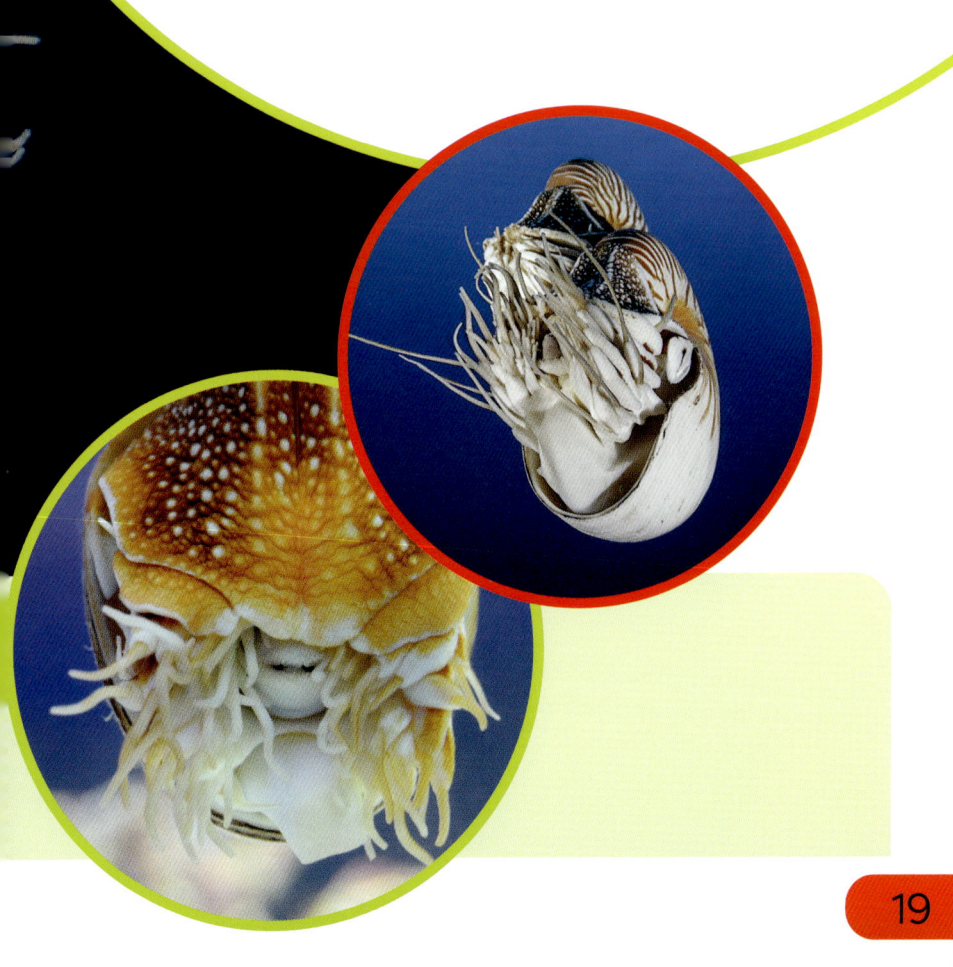

Stinky slime covers
this fish.
The slime tastes bad.

mandarinfish

That way other animals will not eat this fish.

decorator crab

Dress like this crab.
Put on some rocks.
Put on some shells.
Now no one
can see you.

These fish ride on a ray.
The ray keeps
the fish safe.
The fish keep the ray
clean. Hang on!

remora fish

manta ray

Hide with a horse.
A seahorse
of course.

seahorse

Jump and play.
It is the best part
of the day.

dolphin

Splash down.
Then jump again.

You did it!
You jumped. You ate.
You played like
an ocean animal.

Glossary

dolphin
a mammal that lives in the sea

frogfish
a fish that blends in with rocks or other things to hide

nautilus
a sea animal related to octopus and squid

seahorse
a fish that hides in coral

sea turtle
an animal that hatches on land, then grows up in the sea

Quiz

Answer the questions to see what you have learned. Check your answers with an adult.

1. How does the jelly move?

2. What animal has a shell?

3. Which fish stinks?

4. What animal puts on shells and rocks?

5. How do the fish help the ray?

1. The wind pushes it 2. Nautilus 3. Mandarinfish 4. Decorator crab 5. The fish keep the ray clean